# Co-Existing

## Kingsley A. Ndukwe

authorHOUSE®

*AuthorHouse™ UK Ltd.*
*500 Avebury Boulevard*
*Central Milton Keynes, MK9 2BE*
*www.authorhouse.co.uk*
*Phone: 08001974150*

*First published by AuthorHouse 07/14/2011*

*ISBN: 978-1-4567-7449-3 (sc)*

# INTRODUCTION

Making peace between cats and dogs, is co-existence possible?

How can we get our cats and dogs live together in our homes?

Cat meets dog, can they live together peacefully?

The odd couple: cats and dogs, can they be friends?

Re-homing cats with dogs, can that work?

All these questions and more led to this fascinating book 'CO-EXISTING'.

Are you thinking about adopting a perky little puppy as a friend for your fluffy cat, but worried they will fight,- well like cats and dogs?

As a student of Behavioral Science from one of the world's renowned universities, I have struggled for years to find answers to these questions. It has taken a lot of efforts to search through reliable and empirical materials in order to address the questions raised.

This book is written with a great deal of attention to pet lovers, owners and those intending to own a cat or dog or those still undecided on whether to own both.

This book never lost sight in realizing that that we are an animal- loving society where so many families have adopted a cat/s or dog/s and treated them equally as cherished members of our homes. It is important to remember that we are discussing about man's best friends – (Cat and Dog). Hence it is noteworthy to realize that over 30% of the UK population currently own dogs. This equates to 6.8 million dogs. The source of this information is kgb agent which was released on the 21$^{st}$ of May 2010, which seemed to be the most current. It is also believed that over 44% of the UK population have a pet which equates to 9.68 million. Of these, 6.8 million are dogs. Sources from Pamela a kgb agent had it that as at 12$^{th}$ of April, 2007, there are approximately 1.28 million male cat owners and 4.7 million female cat owners. The majority of those live in London. This same source claimed that as at this period, we had over 6.8 million dogs in the UK. There are so many reliable sources to look at, but would prefer not to bore you with so much information. UK domestic dog population is larger than originally thought which was posted by K9 Magazine News Editor on 6$^{th}$ February, 2010, in Dog News. Also a new study also hinted that cats and dogs are the most popular pets in the UK. The same applies to the United States of America but where 23% either own a dog or a cat. There are no wide disparities in the figures obtained from countries like Australia, Canada, France, Germany and New Zealand.

This therefore gives you an idea about the magnitude of the subject we are dealing with here and therefore to be taken seriously. Therefore ensuring that there is a great amount of harmony existing among our pets remains of paramount importance in this book.

The age long relationship between the cat and the dog has generally not been peaceful. They are usually seen as the pair that cannot see eye to eye. Even when humans fight or quarrel, it has always been described to as fighting 'like cats and dogs and in the same when it rains non-stop, this is said to be raining cats and dogs.

This notion that put the cat and dog in bad light as if they are neighbors that cannot tolerate each other prompted this book which will prove that irrespective of their ancestry background and genetic make-up, both can live together peacefully if we can strive to meet some important conditions which will be discussed in great detail. Always remember that most dogs can be taught to tolerate cats if their owners are willing to be patient and consistent in their training. Some dogs may take a longer time to train than others and so many other factors that shall be looked into. Hence for a clearer understanding of this two, 'CO-EXISTING' will delve into their origin and types and then be able to demonstrate that if the right conditions are met, there is no reason why they cannot live in harmony in our homes.

# THE ORIGIN OF CATS

Cats have always generated great deal of interests and a source of fascination for humans throughout history. Today's cats have become one of the world's most popular pets completely suited to the lifestyle of our day. They are beautiful, enigmatic and easy-to-care pets. But then the lingering question remain; Where and when did the domestic cats originate?

The origin of cats has not been as straight- forward as most people thought because there are so many writers and scholars with divergent views on this subject.

It has been suggested that cats were first domesticated about 4000 years ago by the ancient Egyptians to control vermin and other pests and also to protect stores of food. The ancient Egyptians view of the cat was that of a hunter. They were also revered. In those days, it carries a death penalty for killing cats and their bodies mummified before burial could take place.

Domestic cats till date still share many of their attributes from their wild ancestors, that is the wild cats such as the lions and tigers This could be seen in the following physical features such as the body shapes, the arresting eyes, feeding, grooming and the ability to pounce into action at slightest opportunity are the things that make the domestic cat such a fascinating animal around the world.

The wild cat of today such as the tigers and lions, all carnivores, share ancestry lineage called the miacids. From the miacids emerged these three types of modern wild cats such as the Asiatic desert cat, the European wild cat and the African wild cat. The domestic cat originated from the African wild cat because of its tabby markings.

Because of man's interest for the domestic cats, other ancient civilizations started domesticating them and hence some ended up in Italy, where they were further taken to some, if not all parts of Europe and the western world. Some were said to have arrived various destinations through pilgrims and the short-haired spread across the world through Egypt, while the long-haired came from Iran and Turkey. The domestic cat also spread from India to Japan and China. The most popular of the domestic cat which is non pedigree is the 'Moggy', which is normally black and white. The Black cat remains the second favorite and followed by the tabby cat.

Brian Herdwerk, writing for the National Geographic News insisted that the domestic cat could be traced to Middle Eastern wild cat ancestors. All the various authors and writers have all come to agree on one thing about the domestic cat; they originated from the wild cat ancestors. The Eastern wild cat still wanders the desert of Israel and Saudi Arabia and other Middle Eastern countries. It is still believed that between 70,000 to 100,000 years ago, the animal gave rise to the genetic lineage that eventually produced the domestic cats. 'It is plausible that ancient (domestic cats) lineages were present in the wild cat population' asserts Brian Herdwick. Another line of thought had it that wild cats may have been captured about 10,000 to 12,000 years ago when humans started farming.

A research team led by a geneticist Carlos Driscoll of the National Cancer Institute and scientists at the University of Oxford, United kingdom found five matriarchal lineages to which the modern domestic cats belong. 'This also tells us that domestic cats were sort of widely recruited probably over time and space. But people were not just going out and catching them, the cats domesticated themselves. People today know you cannot keep a cat inside without a barrier and 10,000 years ago in the Fertile Crescent you could not just shut the window'. The Science journal also lends its support to the fact domestic cats around the world can trace their origin back to the Middle East Fertile Crescent. At least five female ancestors from the region gave birth to all the domestic cats alive, scientists believe.

# ARCHEOLOGICAL EVIDENCE

The earliest archaeological evidence of cat domestication dates back to 9,500 years ago when cats were thought to have lived along side humans in settlement sites in Cyprus. Domestic cats are generally thought to be offspring of the old world wild cats but differ from these hypothesized progenitors in behavior in tameness and coat color diversity. Ancestors of domestic cats are now thought to have broken away from their wild relatives and started living with humans as early as 130,000 years ago.

# THE DNA EVIDENCE

The researchers focused on the DNA in the mitochondria, the power- plant of cells which supply energy and have their own genetic materials. Comparison of the genetic sequence enabled researchers to determine the relationship between different cat lineages. They found that cats fell into distinctive genetic groups. The results show that apart from accidental cross breeding, European wild cats are not part of the 'moggy''s ancestry. Neither are the Central Asian wild cat, the Southern African wild cat or the Chinese Desert cat. 'But the domestic cats formed a clade with some wild cats from the Middle East, suggesting that today's moggy stems from the wild felines of this region.

Experts still believed that cats originally sought out human company, attracted by rodents infesting the first agricultural settlements. The early farmers of the Fertile Crescent present day Iraq, Syria, Lebanon and Israel would have found the animals extremely useful for protecting their crops and stores, an association that carries on till date.

# THE ORIGIN OF DOGS

The origin of the domestic dog, (Canis Lupus Familiaris) started with the domestication of Gray wolf (Canis Lupus) several tens of thousand years ago.

Domesticated dogs provided humans with a guard animal, a source of food through hunting, fur and beast of burden. The process continues to this day as the international cross-breeding of dogs progressed to date into what we now know as the 'Designer Dogs'.

In terms of domestication of dogs, it can be said that the earliest fossil carnivores that can be linked with some certainty to canids are the Eocene Miacids dating back to about 38 million years ago. The cat-like (Feloidea) and the dog-like (Canoidea) carnivores evolved from the miacids. Most important to the ancestry of the dog was the Canoid line ,leading from coyote-sized Mesocyon of the Oligocene (some million years ago) to the fox-like 'Leptocyon' and the Wolf-like 'Tomarctus' that wandered North America some 10 million years ago. From the time of Tomarctus, dog-like carnivores have grown in population throughout the world.

For a good understanding of the origin of the dog, we shall approach it through different school of thoughts namely;

Archaeological Perspective
DNA Evidence
Possible Routes
Experimental Viewpoint

# ARCHAEOLOGICAL PERSPECTIVE

Archaeologists have suggested that the earliest known domestication of dogs at about 30,000 BC and with certainty at 7000 BC. Evidence has also shown that dogs were domesticated at East Asia. Domestication of the wolves over a period of time resulted in a number of physical changes resembling those that are found in mammals. These changes are prominent in the following areas; shrinking in the size of teeth, reduction in brain size and intelligence and thus in cranial capacity (particularly those areas that have a lot to do with sensory processing and alertness necessary in the wild and the pronounced 'stop' or vertical drop in front of the forehead Brachycephaly). Behaviorally, the wagging of tail and barking are still behaviors only found in wolf puppies, retained via neoteny throughout the dogs' life. Certain wolf-like behaviors such as the regurgitation of partially digested food for the young are no longer existent.

# DNA EVIDENCE

Before the emergence of the DNA evidence, researchers had to deal with two divergent views;

Firstly, it was suggested that the early dogs were descendants of tamed wolves, which interbred and evolved into a domesticated dog.

The second was based on the idea that even though the wolves were thought to be the main player never ruled out that the jackals or coyotes had a lot to dog's ancestry.

Carles Vila, who carried out so many extensive researches to date has ruled out any ancestors to canine species except the wolf. Vila with other researchers analyzed 162 examples of wolf DNA from 27 populations in Asia, North America and Europe. The results were compared with DNA from 140 individual dogs from 67 breeds gathered from around the globe. Using blood/hair samples, DNA was collected and genetic distance for mitochondrial DNA was estimated between individuals.

Based on the DNA evidence, most of the domesticated dogs were found to be members of one of the four groups. 'the largest and most diverse group contains sequences found in the most ancient dog breed, including the Dingo of Australia, the New Guinea Singing Dog and many modern breeds like the Collie and Retriever. Other groups such as the German Shepherd showed a closer relation to wolf sequences than those of the main dog group, suggesting that such breeds had been produced by crossing dogs with wild wolves'.(Wikipedia - the free encyclopedia.)'Vila is still uncertain whether domestication happened once- after which domesticated dogs bred with wolves from time to time_ or whether it happened more than once.'

There were so many researches carried out in this area, prominent among them is the one by Peter Savolainen and others identified DNA evidence suggesting a common origin from a single East Asian gene pool for all dog populations

# EXPERIMENTAL EVIDENCE

The 'Farm-Fox' experiment, apparently another experiment into the domestication of wolves was carried out by a Russian scientist called Dmitry Belyaev. He and his associates tried to show how domestication may have taken place. Working with selectively breeding wild silver foxes over thirty five generations and forty years for the sole purpose of friendliness to humans, created more dog-like animal. ' The domestic- elite foxes' are much more friendly to humans and actually seek human attention, they also show new physical traits that parallel the selection of tameness, even though the physical traits were not originally selected for. They included floppy ears, earlier sexual maturity, barking vocalization, spotted or black and white coats etc. It was reported that 'on average the domestic foxes respond to sounds a couple of days earlier than the non domesticated ones. More striking is that their socialization period has greatly increased. Instead of developing a fear response at 6 weeks of age, the domesticated foxes don't show it until 9 weeks of age or later.

# TYPES OF CATS

## PERSONALITY, TRAITS

There are different types of cats. Different cat breeds have their distinctive characteristics. For example some cat breeds have long tails while some have short tails.

The following are the list of some cat breeds;

### BALINESE CAT

Balinese cats are inquisitive, clever and lively. They have blue eyes, long hair, four colors, lilac point, chocolate point and seal point. Their heads are wedge shaped.

## SOMALI CAT

The Somali cat is a long haired cat breed that weighs between 7 to 12 pounds. It has a soft coat and the eyes are hazel or amber. They normally have a lively and active personality.

## HIMALAYAN CAT

Himalayan cat is a large breed which is also known as 'Color Point Persian'. It has a round head and short nose and vivid blue eyes. It weighs about10 to 13pounds. They are not overly active.

## JAVANESE CAT

The Javanese cats are also known as the 'oriental long hair'. They are very nimble and playful. They have long silky coat, long tail, high cheek bone and slightly almond shaped eyes.

# PERSIAN CAT

Persian cats are the most popular of all cat breed especially in England and the USA. It is a gorgeous breed. The head is round, the nose is short, eyes are large and round, and weighs about 7 to 15 pounds.

# SHORT HAIR TYPE CATS

They are as follows;

Bengal, Manx, British short hair, California, Spangled cat, Russian Blue, Havana Brown, Abyssinian. Other cat breeds include the Norwegian forest cat, snowshoe, Turkish Van, Scottish fold, Ragdoll, Siamese, Siberian, Maine Coon, Tiffany, Turkish Angora, Egyptian Mau, European Burmese, Cornish Rex, Burmese cat, American Short Hair, American Wire Hair, American Bob tail, Selkirk Rex, Exotic Short hair and the list goes on and on.

# BENGAL CATS

Bengal cats are active, sometimes almost doglike in their behavior. They are very loving, affectionate and intelligent. They like to fetch, chew, go for walk and play with you. They can be naughty when they are bored, opening cupboards and fridge doors and rampaging through the contents, sinking their teeth into anything they consider food or edible. They could bite a plastic milk carton and through which they could drink the milk. This goes to suggest the extent they could go in search of food and intelligence. They have the tendency of playing with water, like drinking from the tap and from the toilet if you forget to put the lid down. They paw the top of their water bowl before drinking almost as if they have to brush leaves out of the way. They will sometimes join in the shower and enjoy watching you bathe from the side of the bath. They will like to be with you at all times and will always complain loudly if shut outside the room. They are athletic and can jump very high (ground to top of door frame). They sometimes use their front paws to grasp things as well as claw at them. Some will even attempt at holding a spoon. Some will cuddle on your lap and purr loudly, while others may choose to sit near you and smile with their eyes. They can be quite talkative and always reply when you speak to them.

## MANX — CAT BREED

The Manx cat is huggable, an almost audible meow and a naughty twinkle in its eyes. It spends every waking moment investigating its world. A Manx will gravitate to the centre of your home and insist upon being a member of your family. It possesses an uncanny ability to adapt itself to the psychological needs of its owners. In a home with children who have been taught gentle animal care, they are often in the children's play room, actively supervising the movement of dump trucks and doll carriages. Breed is definitely not for anyone who wants a beautiful feline house ornament. While Manx can fulfill the beauty requirements, it can never be content to serve as a doorstop or window decoration.

# TYPES OF DOGS

There are over 157 different types of dogs recognized by the American Kennel Club. This section will help some of our readers wishing to adopt a dog as to which one that will suit their individual needs.

## DOGS FOR THE DEAF/BLIND - HEARING DOG

These are trained dogs that serve as ears for their mute and deaf owners. Their trainers teach them to differentiate among various types of sounds and re-act accordingly. Little wonder then about the reference of dog as man's best friend especially to people with disabilities who have been rescued in times of grave danger and also their main and loyal companion.

## THE IRISH RED SETTER

This is a lovable and a great family dog, which wants to please every one and loves to be pleased and would be easily heartbroken if owners do not reciprocate his kind hearted nature. Therefore owners as well as those wishing to adopt him, be reminded of its sensitive nature. Trainers are to remember also to handle them with care and utmost gentleness.

## THE WELSH CORGI DOGS

The Welsh Corgi Dog belongs to the herding group and which has always been of great assistance to humans in terms of providing food. They are among the most popular breed pets.

## THE CHOW- CHOW

Is a breed of dogs originating in China. The Chow-Chow or the Puffy Lion dog was derived from the translation of Chinese sounds. They are very friendly and lovable with owners, however not the same kind of treatment to strangers who are not welcome in his property.

## THE AUSTRALIAN CATTLE DOG

They are robust and extremely active and exceptionally gifted herd dog and a great watch dog. As a pet, this great-heart dog makes everyone around fall in love with him.

## THE OTTER HOUND

This is a rare and big dog that will always protect you. Notable among its features are his loud bark and strong personality mixed with his loving and happy nature. Because of his size, it is advised that owners provide him with large space. More so, because of its rarity, the Otter hound is counted among the endangered species.

# THE COLLIE

The Collie is the embodiment of that charming lessie personality. It has the royal elegance, the witty intelligence plus incredible and total reflection of loyalty. It is all you can possibly ask for in a dog

# THE PIT BULLS

This very name stirs controversy. So what is funny? Some see them as aggressive, fighters and nuisance to the society and has been mentioned frequently in the use of illegal dog fights. Simply put, it is common knowledge that the 'Pit bull' breed was developed for blood sports as there are Bull baiting, bear baiting and dog fighting. They are built for performance, a medium sized, short coated and very muscular. Its main characteristics include the following; typical strong body frame with a deep chest, brick-like head, the jaws strong and wide, ears may be cropped or not and also equipped with powerful and proportionate hind end and solid legs and the overall impression is that of power and athleticism. This is not a dog for couch potatoes as it requires loads of training and exercise on a regular basis. This breed requires early training, to be taught to sit and greet people calmly as its natural behavior will be to climb into their lap, put a paw on each of their shoulders and attempt to wipe their face off with its tongue and any attempts to convince a full grown pit bull that it is too big to be a 'lap dog' in most cases fall on deaf ears if they are not taught manners at early stage of life as a puppy.

## ROTTWEILER

There has been this notion of the American and German Rottweiler. The American Rottweiler is said to be taller and leggier while they claim the German Rottweiler is said to be stockier, shorter and have a bigger blockier head. Critics have argued that this is an absolute garbage as there is one and only universal Rottweiler.

The Rottweiler has a muscular, powerful and massive body. The head is broad with a rounded forehead. A Rottweiler is known to have blue eyes or one brown and the other blue. Among other features are; the wide black nose, black lips and inside the mouth dark, the medium sized eyes are dark and almond shaped. The ears are triangular, customarily docked. The coat is short, hard and thick. It is black with rust to mahogany markings on the cheeks and muscle, paws and legs. There also exists a red color with brown markings. His chest is broad and deep. The Rottweiler is a powerful, calm and intelligent breed that is devoted to their owner and family. This breed requires an owner that is strong minded, calm but firm and able to handle this big frame. They are highly intelligent and little wonder they have always been deployed in police, customs and military departments round the world over hundreds of years. Training is also advised when they are still puppies because of their massive size.

## THE BORZOI- THE RUSSIAN WOLF HOUND

Big and playful, the Borzoi or the Russian wolf Hound as it is called is a great hunter and very intelligent and the fun is always guaranteed.

## THE CURLY COATED RETRIVER

You don't require any fear to own it as a pet. He is so friendly and intelligent and will surely bring joy to the home.

## THE OLD ENGLISH SHEEP DOG

Big and fluffy, full of joy and energy, the Old English Sheep Dog or the 'Bobtail' is a dog with over 200 years of history.

The list of types of dogs is endless but vital questions every prospective owner would always ask in choosing a family dog are;

Which breed would suit the purpose for which they are adopted?

Which breeds are good for children?

Have I got adequate knowledge of its traits?

What are their health problems and allergies?

Is treatment easily available and affordable?

Can I adhere to its nutritional needs?

Have I got enough space and time to care for it?

These and many other questions need to be addressed in order that we experience a lasting and wonderful relationship with our pets.

# CATEGORISATION OF THE TYPES OF DOGS

## SPORTING DOGS

Sporting dogs, which are made up of 26 different types of dogs. These types of dogs are usually alert and attentive. This makes them well likable and over all they have good character and personality. Dog breeds within this group are the Retrievers, Spaniels, Setters, Pointers etc.

## HOUND DOG

A good proportion of the hounds share an ancestry involved with hunting, often used by noblemen some years ago. Many have excellent sense of smell, keen eyes and good stamina. Among this group comprise of the Beagles, Greyhound, Harrier, Irish -Wolfhound, Borzoi, Basset Hound and Afghan Hound, etc. Those intending to keep them as pets and owners will need plenty of space and ensure there is enough exercise for them.

## NON SPORTING GROUP

This type of dog is often varied and diverse. Dog breeds in this group include the Boston terrier, Dalmatian and the chow-chow. Due to their diversity, it is difficult to place them into a personality or describe their overall character. With varied coats, function and sizes, this group of dogs has something for everyone. The non sporting group is also known as the utility group, because they are a wide variety or collection of dogs in a complete range of sizes, personalities, coat types and overall appearances. They were classified as non-sporting because they were previously considered as dogs that did not hunt. They include the following; French Bulldog, Dalmatian, American Eskimo Dog, Chow-

Chow, Tibetan Spaniel, Finnish Spitz, Keeshond, Poodle(Miniature and standard) etc.

## TERRIER GROUP

The terrier group is known to be feisty and were bred to tirelessly hunt vermin both below and above ground. They are very often thought of as the 'pest controllers' of the dog world. They undertake active jobs and therefore require regular training. They are the following, Australian Terrier, Scottish Terrier, Parson Russell Terrier, bull Terrier, Norwich Terrier, Skye Terrier, Norfolk Terrier, Irish Terrier, Kerry blue Terrier, Fox Terrier (Smooth and Wire), Lakeland Terrier, Manchester Terrier, etc. Please note that terriers make great pets, however, they do need owners that have matching strong personalities. Hence if you are thinking of adopting an alert, playful, and affectionate dog, then any member of the terrier family might be the right choice.

# WORKING DOGS

Working dogs assist humans in different tasks, from guarding to tracking, to pulling carts, to water rescue. They were originally bred to assist man in very specific and practical ways. They are usually associated with guiding, pulling, leading, guarding, protecting and saving lives. Presently, they act as our companions as they have become integral part of our society. Their popularity has increasingly grown with humans due to their active minds, trainability and willingness to work. This breed needs to be kept occupied in order to keep them happy and fulfilled. Many of this may not make the most suitable pets for 'regular' families due to their strength and size, hence a lot of training are required for them. Types of dogs in this group are; Rottweiler, Black Russian Terrier, Boxer, mastiff, Bull mastiff, Saint Bernard, Akita dog, Great Dane, German Pinscher, Portuguese Water Dog, Siberian Husky, Alaskan Malamute, Newfoundland, etc

# HERDING DOG GROUP

They are bred for stamina and will work with their owners, long hours of the day in their farms or fields without tiring. They are trained to take verbal commands from a distance. They were bred primarily to help farmers drive their livestock and keep them under control even when there is no human supervision. The agricultural lands all over the world may never have been settled as we know them today without the help of the herding dogs. They include the following; The Belgian sheep dog, Polish lowland sheep dog, Welsh corgi, Australian cattle dog, Bearded collie, Australian shepherd, Old English sheep dog, German Shepherd, etc.

# MISCELLANEOUS GROUP

There are many different dog breeds in the miscellaneous group, all of which are awaiting the final breed recognition by the American Kennel Club (AKC). All of these breeds in this group can compete and earn titles in AKC obedience, Tracking and agility events. The type of dogs in this group are the following; Icelandic Sheepdog, Leonberger, Bluetick Coonhound, Boykin Spaniel, Norwegian Lundehund, Redbone Coonhound, Treeing Walker Coonhound, etc.

## TOYS

The sole purpose of the Toy dog is to keep their owners happy due to their small size and excellent health. They could be called our little companions or 'lap dogs'. Many of this breed came from Asia where the process of selectively breeding dogs to make them smaller and smaller is believed to have originated. Nonetheless, there are many other small breeds from other parts of the world. They became very popular during the middle ages. They would be held and carried around by their owners so that the fleas which were so prevalent at this time would be transferred to the toy dog rather than to their owners. They are quite tough and resilient in their nature irrespective of their small size. Dogs in this group are the Chihuahua (Smooth and Long coated), Maltese, Pug, Italian greyhound, Miniature Pinscher, Japanese chin, English Toy Dog (Blenheim and Prince Charles, King Charles and Ruby.), Toy

Manchester Terrier, Pekingese, Brussels Griffon, Chinese Crested, Silky Terrier, Yorkshire Terrier, Japanese Chin and many others.

There are many different types of dogs with well over150 recognised breeds as well as many more variants. Amongst these are the most popular ones that are common in the United Kingdom and the United States of America.

In the UK are the Labrador Retriever, Yorkshire Terrier, German Shepherd, (Alsatian), Beagle, Golden Retriever, Dachshund, Boxer, Poodle, Miniature Schnauzer, Shih Tzu while in the USA, we have the Labrador Retriever, Cocker Spaniel, Boxer, Golden Retriever, English Springer spaniel, Staffordshire bull terrier, German Shepherd or the Alsatian as sometimes called, Cavalier King Charles Spaniel, Border Terrier and West Highland White Terrier. It is noteworthy to realize that when choosing a dog to also examine your personal circumstances, (for instance, home life and how much time available for the dog and the children) and juggle them with a dog who has the appropriate temperament and requires the level of care that you can provide. Here are some questions that need addressing before you can adopt your pet;

How much space do you have?

What size is good?

How much exercise and time do you have for the dog?

Where will the dog live?

How much grooming do you want to do?

Do you have the experience to deal with a more challenging dog?

If you have kids, how will the dog be with them?

Do you have the resources to keep your dog or pet?

These and other vital questions will definitely call for your attention and actions.

# CO-EXISTING
# HOW CAN WE GET THE DOG AND CAT
# LIVE PEACEFULLY IN OUR HOMES?

## THE ODD COUPLE

Many questions have been raised as to whether the dog and cat can live peacefully in our homes. They have also been described as the odd couple, can they ever be friends? Is co-existence possible?

It is in the light of the above that this book has chosen to look at the following;

i)      The origin of cats

ii)     The origin of dogs

iii)    Types of cats

iv)     Types of dogs - Dog types/ breeds/groups.

'They fight like cats and dogs' is an age-long saying and a common phrase for a good reason. Cats and Dogs have been 'enemies' for a very long time. However not all cats and dogs fight, which can be seen around so many homes across the globe. In order to prevent or reduce the tug of war between this two, a few steps have been taken in this book to bring about conflict resolution.

First, it is very important for your pets to know each other at an early stage of their lives. It has been discovered that the younger your pets are when introduced, the better they will get along very well. Younger pets often are not as territorial of their space as older ones. However, it will also help if one of them has a better house training before the other is introduced as this would go a long way in making life a lot easier for you, the owner.

Also of importance is the need for the initial separation of this two when beginning the introduction process. It is a good idea not to put the two together. Keep them in separate areas in the house, so that they can get used to sound and smell of the other. Also when you move from one pet area of your house to another, always ensure that you let your pet sniff your hands and clothes. This is another way of letting your pet get used to the other's smell. After a few days when they are used to one another's smell, we can finally bring them together or introduce them. Bearing in mind that cats only primary defense against larger predators is flight and dogs are pre- programmed by their ancestry tendencies to chase smaller creatures and have fun doing so, hence the suggestion that the dog is left on the leash so that it will be controlled, and the cat able to escape at any time if necessary. It is also advised that you do not force the two to interact straight-away. Your cat might be a lot comfortable watching the dog from the table-top, while the dog might not show any interest whatsoever in the cat. If that is the most comfortable thing at the moment, just let it be that way. Some have suggested that you can get your friend to bring the cat a few steps closer and if your dog continues to stay quiet at your side, wonderful. Praise him for it. If it attempts to jump at the cat, give him a stern fierce sounding, 'No! Leave it alone'. And a short, sharp jerk on the leach and put him in the 'Sit -Stay' position. Praise him as he continues to sit in this position. Continue to bring the cat closer, a few feet at a time, repeating the corrections as required and ensuring to praise the dog when he sits quietly and ignoring the cat. Have patience, depending on the intensity of your dog, you might only be able to gain a few feet each session. Keep this session repeated from time to time until you have established some sort of familiarity between the pair. When the dog is able to sit calmly even when the cat is right next to him, you are then to proceed to another level. Release the dog from his sit-stay position and let him walk around the room with the cat present. Leave his leach on so that you can easily grab him and give the necessary corrections if he gives any signs of wanting to chase the cat. Your supervision at this point is crucial. To be effective, you must be able to correct the dog each and every moment he thinks about going after the cat. If the dog attempts to chase the cat even once, the tendency that that he will try that again is there, hence the need to start the training sessions afresh. Some dogs learn quicker than others, others may take a longer time to become trust-worthy around cats. Until you are sure the dog will remember his training, don't leave them together unsupervised. Even at this stage, always ensure that there is an escape route for the cat should the dog loose his cool.

Another technique which most owners use that is often practicable to help dogs adjust to a new born baby in the household which has also been applied to a new cat. By giving the dog extra attention and even special treats when the baby or cat is in the room, the dog soon learns that that having them around means very good things are going to come his way.

A Siberian husky owner combined a dog crate with the 'Leave It' command to help introduce her cat and dog. Sometimes the dog was crated while the cat is free in the room and at other times the cat was crated while the dog was left walking free in the room. The dog was allowed to investigate the cat but not to harass or bark at it.

Separating what belongs to each of them and maintaining their individual space is another effective way of making your cat and dog live peacefully in our homes. Always ensure that your cat has its litter box, food, toys and scratching post in a separate area where your dog will not be able to get at them. Also note that our cats and dogs are very wonderful pets but at the same time have their strong personalities and territorial feelings, and once we adhere to this, the more we are likely to bring lasting peace between them.

Another group of researchers believe that introducing a new dog to the home if you have cats or a new cat to a home that is already got a dog can be problematic. However, it is not impossible providing you have the right combination of dog and cat. The personalities of each are very important. 'Gentle, sweet- natured or lazy dogs are more likely to be good with cats than a strong-willed, active and alert dogs. Strong-willed cats that stand their ground and hiss and spit or swipe with a paw are more likely to cope with a new dog than the timid sort that run from everything' says Gwen Bailey who has done a brilliant work on dog and cat behavioral problems.

Like already mentioned, some dogs have a high predatory drive and cannot be trusted with any small, fast moving creature. Some grey hounds are like this and many terriers whose recent ancestors were bred to catch and kill small animals. Terriers especially Jack Russell who have not been socialised with cats when young rarely settle with cats or trusted with them. Hounds, whose requirement for games of chase is high, can also torment cats if they have not grown up with them. Dogs bred for herding also enjoy chase games with cats, but they are more easily controlled. Therefore, as a cat owner who wants to have a dog, never choose a stray or the ones you don't know their history. Find out if the dog is used to living with cats and also take the advice of the shelter staff on the likelihood of it settling with cats. Hence it is vital that you put the temperament, breed and past history into consideration.

Another warning to those who have more than one dog is that one dog will act as an individual, while two or more will act as a pack which could be very troubling for a new cat. Once you have decided on the new arrival, introduction and early encounters are very important and can make the difference between success and failure.

The most recent approach on the possibility of getting the cats and dogs live in harmony in our homes was the research carried out by the Department of Zoology, Tel Aviv University (TAU) and posted on the 10th of September 2008 which has a perfect recipe for inter-species harmony in our homes. 'Thinking about adopting a perky little puppy as a friend for your fluffy cat but worried they will fight_ well like cat and dog.' Think again. New research at this university, the first of its kind in the world has found a new recipe for success. According to this study, if the cat is adopted before the dog and if they are introduced when they are still young, (less than 6 months for kittens and a year for the dogs) there is high probability that your pets will get along swimmingly. Results from this research were recently published in the journal, Applied Animal Behavioral Science. This is the first time anyone has carried out a scientific research on pets living in the same home, says Professor Joseph Terkel and his fellow researchers, the originator of this study from the Department of Zoology, TAU.

After interviewing almost two hundred pet owners who both own a cat and dog, then video-taping and analysing the animals' behaviour, TAU researchers concluded that cats and dogs can co-habit happily if certain conditions are met. Prof Terkel and his graduate student Neta-li Feurstein discovered that two- thirds of the homes they surveyed reported a positive relationship between their cats and dogs. But this was not without problems as there was a reported indifference between the cats and dogs in 25 % of the homes, while aggression and fighting were observed in 10% of the homes. One reason for the fighting might have been crossed species signals because cats and dogs may not have been able to read each others body cues. For instance, cats tend to lash their tails when mad or angry, while dogs arch their backs. A cat purrs when happy, while a dog wags its tail. A cat's averted head signals aggression, while in a dog, the same position signals submission. In homes where cat/dog détente existed, Prof Terkel observed a surprising behaviour. 'We found that cats and dogs are learning how to talk each other's language. It was surprise that cats can learn how to talk 'dog' and vice versa. What is especially interesting Prof Terkel remarked, is that both cats and dogs have appeared to evolve beyond their instincts, they can learn to read other's body signals, suggesting that the two species may have more in common than was previously suspected. Hence he concluded that once familiar with each other's presence and body language, cats and dogs can play together and may enjoy sleeping together on the same couch. They can easily share the same water bowl and in some cases groom each other. The far reaching implications of this Tel Aviv University research on cats and dogs may well extend beyond our beloved pets, to people who do not see eye to eye, including neighbours, different races, sexes, nations, religious groups, colleagues, classes and even world super powers. He then concluded, 'If cats and dogs can learn to get along, surely humans have a better chance. Obviously this opens up another opportunity into other areas that require exploring.